GERBILS
KW-037

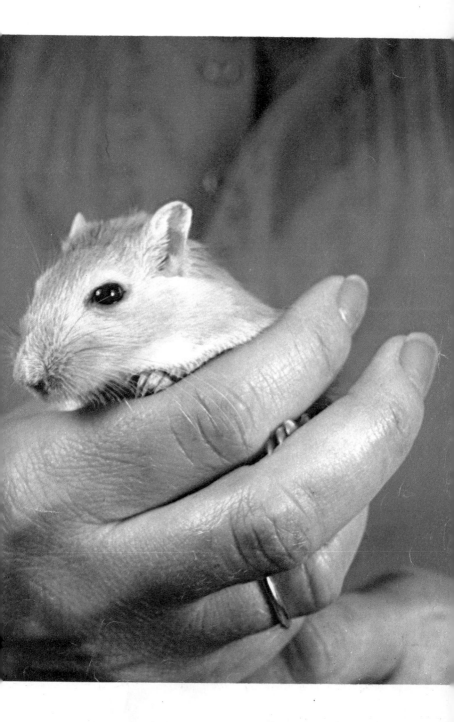

Contents

Introduction—6
What are Gerbils?—10
The Mongolian Gerbil—18
Gerbil Maintenance—34
Handling Gerbils—68
Gerbil Health—80
Breeding Your Gerbils—86
Index—93

Photographers: Glen S. Axelrod, Dr. Herbert R. Axelrod, Michael Gilroy, Ray Hanson, D.G. Robinson, Jr.

Front endpapers: A Mongolian gerbil of the wild or agouti strain. **Title page:** Gerbils are quite capable of standing on two legs when they wish to explore something or when they need to get a better grip. **Back endpapers:** A fancy variety of gerbil.

Distributed in the UNITED STATES by T.F.H. Publications, Inc., One T.F.H. Plaza, Neptune City, NJ 07753; in CANADA to the Pet Trade by H & L Pet Supplies Inc., 27 Kingston Crescent, Kitchener, Ontario N2B 2T6; Rolf C. Hagen Ltd., 3225 Sartelon Street, Montreal 382 Quebec; in CANADA to the Book Trade by Macmillan of Canada (A Division of Canada Publishing Corporation), 164 Commander Boulevard, Agincourt, Ontario M1S 3C7; in ENGLAND by T.F.H. Publications Limited, Cliveden House/Priors Way/Bray, Maidenhead, Berkshire SL6 2HP, England; in AUSTRALIA AND THE SOUTH PACIFIC by T.F.H. (Australia) Pty. Ltd., Box 149, Brookvale 2100 N.S.W., Australia; in NEW ZEALAND by Ross Haines & Son, Ltd., 18 Monmouth Street, Grey Lynn, Auckland 2, New Zealand; in SINGAPORE AND MALAYSIA by MPH Distributors (S) Pte., Ltd., 601 Sims Drive, #03/07/21, Singapore 1438; in the PHILIPPINES by Bio-Research, 5 Lippay Street, San Lorenzo Village, Makati Rizal; in SOUTH AFRICA by Multipet Pty. Ltd., 30 Turners Avenue, Durban 4001. Published by T.F.H. Publications, Inc. Manufactured in the United States of America by T.F.H. Publications, Inc.

GERBILS

PAUL PARADISE

Above: *The Mongolian gerbil is the most commonly bred gerbil for the hobbyist and the laboratory.* **Right:** *Some pet dealers carry other gerbil breeds, such as the rare Egyptian gerbil, which is a much smaller, more ratlike species.*

Introduction

Gerbils may safely be described as virtually ideal pets. They are furry, friendly and easily tamed. They require no special or hard to get foods, and they excrete very little waste, hence they make few demands upon their owners. With more people than ever taking up apartment living, space for pets is becoming very scarce, especially large pets. Gerbils require very little space; in fact, a small cage is all that is necessary in many cases. Gerbils are easily controlled and do not have to be trained to keep off the furniture or out of a particular room.

For the family that would like to have a dog or cat but for reasons of space cannot, gerbils make ideal substitutes. True, they do not show the affection or intelligence

that a dog or cat shows, but as pets they are far superior in many other ways. In cases where allergies prohibit the ownership of fur-bearing pets, gerbils very often can be safely kept, for they barely shed any fur and generally they evoke few allergic reactions in their owners.

Compared to larger animals, gerbils are inexpensive to buy and to keep. Commercial food for gerbils is also inexpensive, and very often gerbils can eat leftover vegetables that you might otherwise discard. It is not necessary to have gerbils altered sexually, for their young take up no additional space and they make no noises that can be heard more than a foot or two away from the cage. It is not necessary to spend any money to board them when you are away; they can be left alone in their cage for quite a few days or their small cage can easily be left with a friend or relative. There is no need to worry about providing them with fresh water very often, for they get most of their water from their food. This also means that their litter does not have to be changed often. Last but not least, gerbils are considered by many to be educational pets, for their interesting burrowing behavior and their innate curiosity can be observed day or night, and they can be handled easily, for they generally do not scratch or bite.

They can even be trained to respond to certain hand signals and noises. Because of their docile nature and because their tail is covered with soft brown fur, most people who are repulsed by the thought of having rats or mice as pets readily take to gerbils as family pets.

Because of its docile nature, clean habits and ease of care, the gerbil, especially the Mongolian gerbil, is rapidly becoming a very popular laboratory research animal too. Its utility in the medical research laboratory lies in its susceptibility to some of the simpler diseases of humans and in its high degree of natural resistance to diseases more easily contracted by most other laboratory rodents.

Opposite: *An adult gerbil can leap nearly two feet in distance. Leaping is generally used as a means of escape, but gerbils may also leap when engaged in territorial fights.*

Above: *Gerbils in the wild live in burrows, which protect them from predators and from the elements. They feed mainly at night in areas close to the opening of the burrow.* **Right:** *A small amount of food will be sufficient to cajole the pet gerbil into eating out of one's hand.*

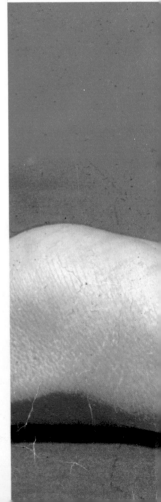

What are Gerbils?

Gerbils are small desert-dwelling rodents that are found in arid regions of eastern Europe, Asia and Africa. They range in size from two inches to ten inches in length and they have a long fur-bearing tail that in most species is almost as long as the body itself.

The name gerbil (pronounced jer-bil, not grr-bil) comes from the Latin word *gerbillus,* meaning "little jerboa." Jerboas are jumping desert rodents that are quite similar to gerbils in size, color and habits. The length of the hind limbs is proportionately longer in jerboas than in most gerbils, and accordingly, their jumping ability is

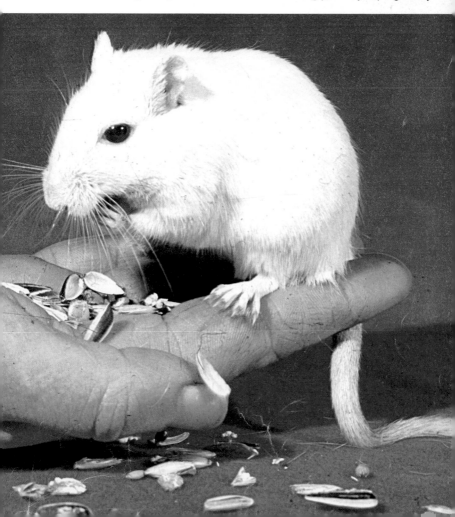

greater. Because of their ability to stand upright on the hind legs, using the tail for balance, and because of their ability to take surprisingly large leaps, jerboas have often been compared to Australian kangaroos. Although the adult gerbil cannot jump quite as adroitly as its relative, the jerboa, it is every bit as adept at standing on the hind legs for the purpose of investigating its environment and for eating as any other desert rodent, and young gerbils jump quite well too.

It is believed that the long tail of the gerbil helps it maintain its balance when it is standing on two legs.

Gerbils are mammals, belonging to the order Rodentia and the family Cricetidae. They are sometimes known as jirds, clawed jirds, pocket kangaroos and sand rats. There are approximately twelve genera of gerbils or gerbil-like rodents belonging to family Cricetidae and there are numerous species within these genera. None of the gerbils except perhaps *Meriones unguiculatus* are well known scientifically, and this is most likely due to the fact that they inhabit some of the most barren and inaccessible places in the world.

It would be quite impossible in a book this size to provide information on all of the rodents known as gerbils, and it's actually not necessary for the purposes of this book. The primary goal here is to provide the reader with as much information as possible on the keeping and breeding of the gerbil known scientifically as *Meriones unguiculatus,* and commonly known as the Mongolian gerbil. It is this particular gerbil species that has become so very popular as a pet in the Western World. Other species of gerbils, however, do occasionally show up in pet shops. They differ somewhat in appearance and in habits from *Meriones unguiculatus,* and it would be helpful for the potential gerbil owner to be able to recognize some of the other gerbils, as he may want to avoid

Gerbils like to gnaw; this practice helps to wear down their ever-growing teeth.

buying anything but the common Mongolian gerbil.

JERUSALEM GERBIL

The Jerusalem gerbil is larger than the Mongolian gerbil, and its color is more reddish. The adult Jerusalem gerbil is about six inches long. This gerbil is native to the Middle East. It has a very nasty disposition and is not of much value as a pet. It becomes frightened when handled and is known to bite. Its habits in the wild are described as usually solitary. Its breeding season lasts from late April to early August. The male usually deserts the female shortly after mating, so family life is matriarchal. The rapidly developing young leave the nest at an early age (three weeks).

EGYPTIAN GERBIL

This is a small species, being no longer than three inches at adulthood. The body is compact and slender, more like a rat's body. The fur is a deep red color except for the standard white belly fur. The ears are proportionately quite large, larger than on any other gerbil species. The Egyptian gerbil is popular because it is a prolific breeder. Its gestation period is 22 to 25 days.

THE LIBYAN GERBIL

The Libyan gerbil is similar in color to the Mongolian gerbil, but it is much more aggressive. It is a light sandy brown color on the back and on the neck. The abdomen is white. Fully grown, this gerbil is eight inches long. The

Opposite top: *A king gerbil. Rodents can move their forearms and digits independently.* **Opposite bottom:** *Before retreating into the burrow, this pygmy, or dwarf, gerbil will cover the burrow's opening with loose sand. Under similar circumstances in nature, a Mongolian gerbil will behave the same way.* **Above:** *An Egyptian gerbil with its young litter. Although they are fully furred, the babies' eyes are still closed.*

tail is nearly as long as the body and it is thick and hairless (most gerbil species have fur-covered tails); the claws are pale in color. In captivity this gerbil is not a good breeder because the female frequently devours her young. The gestation period is about 22 days. This gerbil has the interesting habit of sleeping in a standing or upright position.

INDIAN GERBIL

While the Indian gerbil looks like it might make a good pet, it is a nasty biter. It is very small, measuring just a little over two inches in length. The front and hind paws are hairless. The fur on the back and sides is light brown with some black hairs interspersed among the brown ones.

A female naked-soled gerbil investigating a large jewel beetle. This insect will prove to be inedible, as its wing cases and skin are too hard for rodent teeth to crack.

Gerbils are curious animals that will investigate anything within their reach.

NAMIB PAEBA GERBIL

This gerbil has very large hind feet which have caused it to become known as the snow-shoe gerbil. It is found in northern India and Tibet. Because of its common name, snow-shoe, many people erroneously believe this gerbil inhabits only high altitudes. This, of course, is not true, for its actually found in some of the low-lying areas in its native range. Its elongated toes actually provide it with a great amount of traction on the loose sand in which it lives.

The Namib Paeba gerbil matures to a length of about three inches, with a tail about as long as the body. In the wild this gerbil is an excellent jumper.

The color of the back and head is grayish, but the sides are paler, tending to be a bit reddish in color. The fur of the limbs is white, as is the belly region.

The burrows of this gerbil are difficult to find in the wild, for they are usually covered by sand. The principal predators of the Namib Paeba gerbil are snakes.

PRZEWALSKI'S GERBIL

Przewalski's gerbil is one of the largest known gerbils, measuring nearly eight inches in length. Its fur is thick and coarse, and the fore limbs are hairless. The body is rather heavy-looking and the tail is relatively short. In overall appearance this gerbil looks very much like a rat. Not much is known of its habits, but it is suspected that it may be a burrower, as most gerbils are. This gerbil is found in China and Mongolia, where it is sometimes called the steppe gerbil.

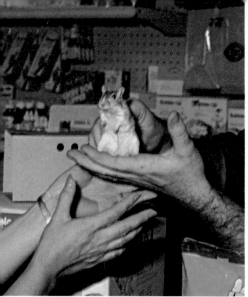

Above: *It is a good policy to handle a gerbil directly prior to its purchase. You will then have a better chance to evaluate its health, appearance, and temperament.* **Right:** *A child's stuffed toy may seem safe for a pet; be sure, however, that such toys are not stuffed with fibers that are harmful to a gerbil's health.*

The Mongolian Gerbil

Throughout the rest of the book, the word gerbil should be taken to mean the Mongolian gerbil. It is the Mongolian gerbil that is most often offered for sale in pet shops.

The existence of the gerbil was unknown in the Western World until the early 1950s when it was discovered by Professor Davidson, a French zoologist. The gerbil was first introduced into the United States in 1954 by Dr. Victor Schwentker at the Tumblebrook Farm, a commercial laboratory animal farm.

The scientific name of the Mongolian gerbil is *Meriones unguiculatus*. *Meriones* was a warrior in Greek mythology and *unguiculatus* means with fingernails.

Mongolian gerbils are not quite

as large as hamsters, but they are larger than most types of domesticated mice. At maturity they may weigh as much as four ounces, but usually they weigh three to three-and-one-half ounces, and the males are a little larger than the females. The total length of a mature adult is usually about eight inches (including the tail) but can be as long as nine-and-one-half inches. A newborn gerbil pup has a tail that is about 25% as long as its body, but the proportion increases as the animal matures, so that at maturity the tail is about 90% of the body length.

The gerbil's color is best described as agouti, which is typical coloration for most desert rodents; many non-desert rodents are also agouti colored. In an agouti animal each hair is white at the base, has a yellowish center band and a black tip. Slight variations can give the animal more of a reddish or a grayish color. Generally, however, the gerbil appears to be reddish tan on the back, head and sides with lighter fur on the feet and toward the underside. The belly fur is white. This coloration suits the animal well in its natural desert habitat, for the white belly helps reflect heat from the desert, which even in Mongolia can be pretty intense during certain days of the year. The agouti sides, back and head provide the gerbil with excellent camouflage, which

protects it against hawks and other predatory birds with which it shares its natural habitat.

There are at least some negative factors in the keeping of any pet. One of the most common is biting, especially among pet rodents such as rats, mice or hamsters. While gerbils certainly aren't perfect (although they're sure close), biting is generally one habit they do not have in common with their rodent cousins. Gerbils are indeed the most docile of all small furry pets! This does not mean they do not bite—I myself have been bitten by gerbils on several occasions. What this does mean is that the gerbil cannot be provoked as easily as any other rodent commonly kept as a pet. Any animal will bite when it is sufficiently irritated, but it usually takes some pretty harsh mishandling to get a gerbil to bite its handler. Hopefully that statement will not encourage mishandling of gerbils, for it is meant only to allay any fear you may have about being bitten by a gerbil—the less fear you have, the easier and safer it is to handle any animal. More will be said about proper and improper handling of gerbils later in this book.

One of the reasons gerbils do not bite is that they are almost fearless—their fright and flight mechanisms are not easily stimulated! In fact, rather than showing fright in response to

Although they have the large eyes that are typical of nocturnal animals, gerbils have periods of activity throughout the day.

Opposite top: *Due to the danger of getting their long tails caught, gerbils should only be given exercise wheels which are designed specifically for them.* **Opposite bottom:** *Note the well developed hindlimbs of this Mongolian gerbil.* **Right:** *Fresh vegetables should be given to gerbils only on occasion, as an overabundance can cause a digestive upset.* **Below:** *When transporting a gerbil in a carrying case, be sure that the case is sturdy and that the animal cannot chew through it.*

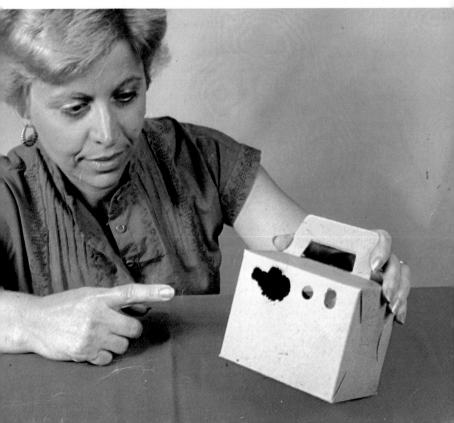

startling stimuli such as sudden loud noises, flashes of light, shadows, etc., gerbils seem to show an innate curiosity. If you walk into a room where a gerbil cage is being kept and make a startling noise such as slamming the door or sneezing loudly, rather than running into their burrows as rats, mice or hamsters might do, gerbils are more likely to stand on their hind legs, balancing themselves on their tail, and look around, perhaps sniffing the air. They seem to want to know what is going on. As a matter of fact, if gerbils are concealed in burrows or other shelters when you come into the room and they are not sleeping, they are very likely to come out of their shelter to greet you. If merely coming into the room does not bring them out, try tapping gently on the cage; that usually does the trick. I've even tried making loud noises, and that rarely fails to bring them out of their shelters. This, of course, does not mean you should walk around the room exploding blown-up paper bags, for in gerbils fear seems to be learned behavior. When their cage is opened, rarely do gerbils run into their shelters or attempt to escape; rather, they usually come out to investigate your hand. They will approach cautiously at first, but at least they will approach, which is more than can be said for most other rodents. Very often they will sniff

the hand at close range, and sometimes they will even lie or sit still while you gently stroke their back or the back of their head with your fingertip. They may even voluntarily climb up onto your hand. Don't worry about getting gerbil droppings on your hand; they rarely do this, and when it is done it is usually only when they are frightened, which, as mentioned earlier, is not very often. Even if they do get droppings on your hand, the droppings are very dry, tiny and hard, so there is no mess, although it's a good idea to wash your hands afterward. In all the years I've handled gerbils I've never had one urinate on my hand, either.

Just exactly why gerbils are so fearless and curious is not definitely known. One can only make some educated guesses here. One idea put forth by people with a knowledge of desert ecology (remember, gerbils are desert animals) is that in the wild gerbils have few enemies, for the areas they live in are usually quite barren. Therefore, in the course of their evolution they probably had no reason to develop strong instinctive fear reactions. Furthermore, gerbils communicate danger warnings throughout the colony by rapidly thumping the rear paws or feet against the hard dry ground they usually live on. This early warning system seems

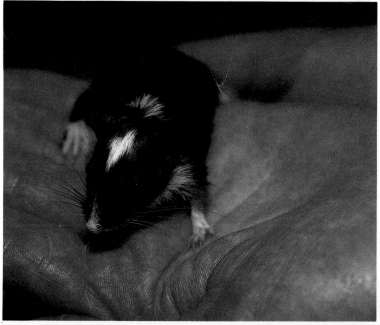

The gerbil is a relatively fearless creature that will explore whenever it gets the chance. As long as the animal is gradually introduced to one's hand, it is most likely that the gerbil will eventually climb into it.

to give all of the other gerbils living in the colony adequate time to hide if real danger is imminent. Apparently their colonial lifestyle and communication system allows them to be curious without placing themselves in great danger very often.

Another interesting and favorable facet of the gerbil's behavior is the noise it makes or, rather, doesn't make. Rarely, if ever, do adult gerbils vocalize. Occasional soft squealing sounds may be heard from juvenile and adolescent gerbils, but these sounds are so soft that one must be practically on top of the cage before they can be heard. Kept in a child's bedroom, the gerbil's loudest vocalization could not very easily disturb a child who is a restless or light sleeper. As adults, gerbils make occasional sounds during courtship or fighting, but these are as inaudible as the squeals of juveniles.

Like most rodents, gerbils gnaw

Opposite top: *Frequent gentle handling enhances trust between gerbils and their keeper.* **Opposite bottom:** *The handling process can begin when you buy your gerbil.* **Above:** *Proper handling and training will be important later, when one wishes to show one's gerbil.*

on almost any object they are given, including even the corners and sides of their cage. The sound thus made can be disturbing, depending upon what kind of material the cage or other object is made of. If gerbils are given pieces of wood or other softer materials upon which to gnaw, they usually ignore the sides and corners of their cage—the sound made when the gerbil gnaws on wood is barely audible. Gnawing is, of course, instinctive behavior in gerbils as it is in most other rodents, and its purpose is apparently to keep the constantly growing incisor teeth sharp and shortened.

Another habit gerbils have is scratching, and usually they scratch the same objects that they gnaw. The scratching is done by very rapidly—almost too rapidly for the human eye to follow—rubbing the front claws in an alternating pattern against the object being scratched in almost a climbing type of motion. This behavior probably serves to keep the nails sharp and shortened in the same way that gnawing does this for the incisor teeth. The loudness of the scratching noise, once again, depends upon the material being scratched. If gerbils are kept in a dry aquarium, it is not uncommon to see them scratching for minutes at a time against the aquarium glass. Scratching and gnawing sounds made by gerbils

are not usually very disturbing to their owners or other people living in the owner's household.

As should be expected of any burrowing animal, gerbils are diggers. They almost constantly attempt to dig into the bottom material in the cage. Whether or not they succeed at digging burrows depends upon the kind of cage and bottom material provided for them. It is interesting to watch a gerbil burrow into the bottom. Supporting itself on the hind legs and using the tail for balance, the gerbil raises itself up, leans forward and, with the front feet, scoops up dirt or whatever material it is digging in and throws it toward the hind legs; then with the hind legs it kicks the dirt out behind it. Watching a gerbil burrow into the bottom material reminds one of a very small dog trying to bury a bone in the back yard. I have seen gerbils dig by alternating the motion of both front feet or by simply scooping with both front feet at the same time. If soft bedding material, such as wood shavings, is being used and a metal or wire cage is the gerbil's home, the digging is almost silent. However, if an aquarium is used as the domicile and dirt as the bottom material, the digging could get a bit rowdy, especially if there are small stones mixed in with the dirt.

While we are on the subject of sounds made by gerbils, this

An array of gerbil colorations. The most common gerbil coat is the natural agouti pattern.

might be a good place to discuss the gerbil's thumping behavior. Thumping in small animals is not as unfamiliar a phenomenon as one might think. Thumping was introduced on a wide scale to the general public many years ago by Walt Disney in a production called *Bambi*. In this story there is a rabbit named Thumper who communicates messages to other animals of the forest by rapidly thumping his hind feet on the forest floor. This idea is not so far-fetched, for rabbits really do thump the hind feet to communicate danger warnings to other rabbits and as a part of the mating ritual.

Gerbils also thump, and they do so for the same reasons as rabbits—to communicate danger warnings to other gerbils living in the colony and as an intricate part of their mating ritual. It is mostly the males that do the thumping. I have even observed this behavior when introducing new gerbils to an already established colony (new gerbils usually are not welcome in an established colony and are often either driven out or killed by the established residents of the colony).

Other activities that can be seen in gerbils are grooming and playing. Because of their minimal urine and feces production, gerbils are extremely clean animals, and another indication of their cleanliness is their frequent grooming behavior. Because of

The stability of a color variety is greatly dependent upon its popularity; breeders produce the color as long as it has a market. **Opposite top:** A Mongolian gerbil with the normal agouti pattern. **Opposite bottom:** A golden gerbil. **Right:** An albino gerbil. **Below:** A black gerbil.

The Mongolian Gerbil

their great suppleness, gerbils are capable of reaching almost any part of the body with the tongue and teeth. Using the teeth and tongue as grooming tools, gerbils may spend up to several hours off and on per day cleaning their own fur. On a few occasions I have even seen gerbils grooming each other.

The dexterity of a gerbil in the use of its forefeet is amazing. To eat, a gerbil usually sits up on its large back legs and grasps and manipulates its food with both front feet, holding the food up to its mouth while it chews away. It can turn the food item in any direction necessary without having to put it down and pick it up again. It also handles twigs, pieces of bark and bedding material in the same way. The gerbil's dexterity with its forefeet seems to be every bit as advanced as that of a squirrel. In fact, when eating in an upright position, the gerbil looks very much like a tiny squirrel. The gerbil can also eat and gnaw while down on all four feet, but if the item being eaten or gnawed upon can be lifted, it seems to prefer the upright position.

Gerbils are not nocturnal animals, nor are they diurnal; rather, they have brief alternating periods of rest and activity throughout the day and night.

However, their activity levels seem to reach a peak at about midnight. They may rest for several hours, then play, burrow, gnaw, scratch, thump, mate and groom for a few hours, and then another rest period follows. Their activities are usually quite intense during their active periods.

Usually one of the first questions the owner of a new pet poses is: how long will my pet live? Gerbils have been known to live in captivity for as long as four years. Some people even claim to have had their pet gerbils for as long as six years. Very often the gerbil's longevity in captivity is much greater than it would be in the wild, especially if it is well cared for. In captivity the gerbil is given all the food and water it needs, so it doesn't have to put up with drafts and food scarcities as it often does in the wild. Furthermore, in captivity there are no hawks and snakes for the gerbil to contend with; these are its principal enemies in the wild. Lastly, even though the gerbil is quite tolerant of harsh variations in temperature and humidity, these variations do take their toll in the wild. In captivity there are no such variations. In captivity, gerbils usually enjoy a good life and live quite long for a small rodent.

Gerbils love to climb. Ladders such as these are available at your local pet shop.
Be sure to purchase ladders that are considered safe for gerbils.

Gerbil Maintenance

HOUSING

After many, many thousands of years of life in the harsh environment of the desert, gerbils have apparently evolved the ability to cope with some pretty radical environmental fluctuations. Accordingly, they can handle some difficult environmental conditions in captivity without showing any apparent ill effects. For instance, a bit of crowding doesn't seem to bother gerbils. One laboratory using gerbils for research recommends a minimum of 180 square inches of floor space for one pair of gerbils and one litter of five to ten pups. That could be a cage having a base that measures, for example, ten by eighteen inches, which is just a bit smaller than the base of a standard ten-gallon aquarium.

A cage about the size of a ten-gallon aquarium may seem a bit cramped for two four-inch-long gerbils and a large litter of pups, but apparently it isn't. However, when the pups are about half-grown (two and a half to three months old) some of them will have to be moved to other quarters, or else the colony will be too crowded. The extra adolescent gerbils can either be given away or sold back to the pet shop that their parents came from; unless, of course, you want to provide them with the required additional housing. At sexual maturity, which occurs at about twelve weeks of age, a single gerbil requires about 36 square inches of floor space. This is equivalent to an area measuring about six inches by six inches. However, gerbils that have just reached sexual maturity still have a good bit of growing to do, and an additional two square inches of floor space per animal for each additional week of age is recommended. Gerbils generally continue to grow until they are eighteen to twenty weeks of age. This means that the 180-square-inch minimum floor space can comfortably house no more than four full-grown gerbils, as long as they are not breeding. Fortunately, when gerbils approach their limit for crowding, rather than fighting and killing one another as some other rodents do, they usually simply stop reproducing. Therefore, there is little need to worry about a gerbil cage becoming badly overcrowded due to excessive reproduction, except, of course, in the case of the first brood. A single pair of full-grown gerbils and one litter, as mentioned before, is not crowded in a ten-gallon aquarium, but if all the pups live and mature, the cage will be badly overcrowded and there probably will be no further successful reproduction. Gerbils have actually been kept and

Opposite: *A pair of gerbils, a light dove and a cinnamon.*

sometimes even bred in much smaller quarters. However, under those conditions the young usually either die of natural causes or are killed by the parents. Also, even a well-matched pair of gerbils is more likely to fight in a crowded or cramped cage than they are in one that gives them plenty of "elbow" room.

As far as cage height is concerned, six inches should be the minimum. This height allows fully matured gerbils to stand upright, as they so often do, without hitting their heads on the roof of the cage. A height of ten or twelve inches is really a little better, since this gives the gerbils more room to jump about when they are playing, battling or mating.

Cage construction should be of a material that is impervious to damage caused by the gnawing and scratching activities of gerbils. Ordinary plastic shoe boxes do not suit gerbils well, for they will gnaw through them in practically no time at all. The same applies to the use of cardboard cages and most wood cages. Heavy plastic cages used by laboratories usually last for quite a while before the gerbils gnaw through them.

A glass aquarium or a metal wire cage is much more suitable than a plastic, wood or cardboard cage, as gerbils cannot gnaw through an aquarium. If an aquarium is chosen, it should be

covered by a large mesh (¼ or ½ inch mesh) screen top. This allows for plenty of fresh air circulation and keeps the gerbils in the tank. Circulation is not a problem with an open cage made of heavy wire or screen mesh. Metal cages, however, should have a solid metal bottom to give the gerbils better footing than they would have on a wire bottom and to allow bedding material to be kept in the cage. The best metal cage is one that has a solid metal back, bottom and ends. In these cages the front is solid metal to a height of two or three inches, and the remainder of the front and the top are generally made of steel wire bars or heavy screen. The solid bottom may be in the form of a removable tray; this facilitates cleaning.

The most popular item used as litter in the gerbil cage is wood shavings. Shavings from almost any kind of wood can be used. Cedar shavings are the most commonly available commercially packaged shavings, and they have a bit of deodorant effect. Even more effective for deodorizing purposes are shavings impregnated with a chlorophyll compound. Deodorant shavings are useful for keeping rats, mice and hamsters, all of which produce considerable amounts of urine, but if gerbils are kept and fed properly, they produce very little urine, so

Two dove gerbils and a cinnamon. Toys such as this plastic shoe are popular with gerbils and their owners. Take care, however, not to crowd the cage with too many furnishings.

deodorant shavings are not really necessary for them. Coarse sawdust is sometimes used as bedding material in small animal cages, primarily because of its absorbency. It is not necessary and should not be used with gerbils. One-half to one inch is the proper depth for the bedding material in the bottom of the cage.

If clean rags or empty toilet paper or paper towel rolls are placed in a bare cage containing a pair of gerbils, the cage will usually contain a suitable amount of shredded bedding material by the next morning, for when in need of bedding and nesting material, gerbils are indeed industrious creatures. They will shred such material within a few hours. If there already is adequate bedding material in the cage, gerbils may not destroy the cardboard rolls right away; rather they will use them as shelters and play tunnels for a while before chewing them up.

If, aside from your interest in gerbils as pets, you also have an academic interest in gerbils, there is a way to set up a gerbil home so that it much more closely simulates the gerbil's natural environment than a metal cage containing wood shavings does. This method requires the use of a fairly large aquarium—a standard 29- or 30-gallon aquarium measuring 30 or 36 inches long and sixteen or eighteen inches high is suitable. If you have an old "leaker" aquarium stored in the attic or in the garage, this is an opportunity to get some use out of it without getting involved in an extensive repair job. It does not need to be absolutely watertight, although any cracked glass panes should be replaced. This is a perfect way to use some of those old metal-framed aquaria that are no longer being manufactured. If you don't have one stored away somewhere, they can often be picked up pretty cheaply at flea markets or at auctions. Even if you can't find an old aquarium of a suitable size, it is worthwhile to invest in a new one, because, except for a cover, you won't need

any of the other aquarium accessories that are normally sold with a new aquarium; therefore, a new tank will not be that expensive. Remember that the tank should be at least sixteen inches in height and higher if possible.

A sturdy cover is needed for this setup. The cover must be sturdy enough to hold up under the stress of daily removal for feeding of the gerbils. It must be made of screen or some kind of wire mesh to permit plenty of air circulation and must fit snugly down over the edges of the tank so that it cannot be accidentally knocked off and allow the gerbils to escape. There are commercially made wire mesh or screen covers that fit standard 29- or 30-gallon aquaria. If your pet dealer doesn't have a suitable cover in stock, he can order one for you.

When setting the aquarium up, make sure it is placed on a firm surface such as a table, for the next step is to place some large, heavy rocks in the tank. If the bottom of the tank is not firmly supported, the rocks could cause it to crack and collapse, unless the tank has a slate bottom, as many of the old metal-framed tanks do. The rocks should be at least six inches in height, and at least two or three of them should be randomly placed in the tank. The purpose of the rocks is to help prevent the tunnels,that the gerbils

Gerbils seem to thrive on toys with entrances and exits. Their adventures are very amusing to watch.

are inevitably going to dig from collapsing.

The next step is to find some suitable soil with which to fill the aquarium. Even though in nature gerbils generally live in a sandy environment, in the aquarium sandy soil will not do, at least not 100% sand. If 100% sand is used, the gerbil's tunnels will collapse, even if the sand is moistened. If collapses occur, the gerbils, especially pups, can be injured or killed. In the wild, gerbils burrow much more deeply into the sand than they can in an aquarium, and at those deeper levels, because it is moister and has some other materials mixed with it, the soil is a lot firmer than it is near the surface. For the aquarium mix, rich garden loam should not be used at all, as it contains a lot of organic material that could become foul in the confines of an aquarium in which there are no plants growing. The ideal material for this setup is finely divided or sifted, fairly dry (but not dusty dry) clay soil mixed with a small amount of sand, a little bit of gravel (1¼-inch particle size) and perhaps a small bit of dry straw. If the additives are not available, use only 100% clay soil. If moisture conditions are properly maintained, tunnels dug in clay soil will not collapse. Before placing the soil into the aquarium it is important that as many of the

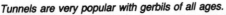

Tunnels are very popular with gerbils of all ages.

A breeding pair of gerbils, dove female and agouti Canadian white spot male.

lumps as possible be broken up. Eventually this will help add more strength to the tunnel walls and ceilings. If the soil is sifted, the lumps will automatically be either broken up or excluded. If the soil is too damp, it will pack down too tightly when it is placed into the tank. The soil should be fairly dry to start with and moisture adjustments can be made later after the soil is in place. It should be dry enough so that it is *not* possible to mold it smoothly into a ball about the size of a baseball, but it should be moist enough so as to not produce any dust when a handful of it is dropped into the aquarium. After you have had a little experience in maintaining this setup, you'll become more familiar with the correct moisture content of the soil.

With several rocks in place, the soil mixture can now be dumped into the aquarium. If the aquarium is sixteen inches high, the final soil depth should be about ten inches, thus retaining a six-inch space between the soil surface and the cover. If the tank is higher, for example eighteen inches, the final soil level can be as high as twelve inches. In other words, no matter how high the aquarium is, always try to maintain a minimum of about six inches of air space over the soil. The soil should be dumped in a few inches at a time and lightly tamped down between each addition. Make sure that all spaces around the rocks are filled with soil. There should be no large air pockets anywhere in the substrate. It is difficult to describe exactly how tightly the soil should be packed down. It should be hard enough to allow the gerbils to burrow into it without having it collapse over them, but it should not be so hard as to make it at all difficult for them to dig into it. With a little bit of experience, like finding correct moisture content, you will soon discover the correct soil hardness.

It is not necessary to put any plants into the soil, for they will be destroyed by the gerbils in short order. We know a person who set up a soil habitat for his gerbils and finished the job by placing a layer of Kentucky bluegrass sod, which he had removed from his lawn, over the entire soil surface. He then introduced four gerbils into the habitat and four hours later was shocked to find all of the sod gone. Not only was the sod gone, but all the gerbils were prostrate on the soil surface, panting quite rapidly. His gerbils had mowed the lawn much closer than could be done by any lawn mower or even by a herd of sheep, and in doing it so quickly they had exhausted themselves! Some of the grass was eaten, but most of it was piled up in one corner of the aquarium and was later used by the gerbils as nesting material once they had dug their burrows. The gerbils, of course, recovered from their ordeal and went on to produce a thriving colony of about twenty healthy gerbils. Any live plants placed into the aquarium will be destroyed by the gerbils just as our friend's bluegrass sod was destroyed.

Maintaining the correct moisture in the soil is not difficult, but if water is not added at least once every few days the soil will become too dry, even if it is being kept in a very moist atmosphere in the home. This condition will, of course, produce dust (unhealthy for you and for the gerbils) and will subject the tunnels to collapse. Water is added to this setup by making it rain very lightly over the entire soil surface. This can be done by using a garden sprinkling can that has a very fine strainer over the spout or by using a finger-operated atomizer pump such as the type used in caring for delicate house plants. How much moisture should be added

Gerbils are territorial animals; it is not uncommon for several breeding pairs and their respective litters to share the same living area. Female gerbils will even help each other with the brooding of pups.

depends upon how dry the atmosphere in your home is. An exact formula cannot be given, but a little experience will teach you how much to add and how often to add it.

Since within a few hours after being placed in the tank the gerbils will already have dug several tunnels, adding water to the dirt must be done as recommended above rather than by just pouring it from a glass tumbler or a watering can lacking a spout strainer. Only a very small amount of water should be added at one time, even if it is necessary to rain several times during the day to get the right amount of water into the soil. If larger amounts of water are added in a heavy downpour the water is very likely to flood the gerbils' tunnels. Most adult gerbils will be able to dig their way out of flooded and possibly collapsed tunnels, but juveniles and newborn pups may drown or suffocate.

To the gerbils it doesn't seem to matter whether they are kept in a metal cage, a box or a soil-filled aquarium. They remain healthy, reproduce and live for a long time in almost any type of setup if they are well cared for. However, there are a few great advantages to the gerbil owner if keeping the gerbils in a soil-filled aquarium rather than in a metal cage or a wooden box. The biggest advantage is that other than an occasional raining on the soil, there is virtually no maintenance required of the gerbil owner for at least six months to a year, depending upon how crowded the gerbil colony becomes. Rarely does such a setup produce any unpleasant odors such as the ammonia smell that develops after a month or so in a metal cage containing wood shavings; in the cage-type of setup the litter must be changed every two to four weeks. Another advantage is that a large soil-filled aquarium evokes in the gerbils more of the kinds of activities that one might see when observing them in the wild—about the only thing missing from this artificial environment is the predators! In addition, the gerbils usually dig some of their tunnels right against the glass sides of the aquarium, so the gerbil keeper often has the opportunity to see how the gerbils behave underground—an experience that a trip to the far reaches of Outer Mongolia would not yield! It is much like observing ants in an artificial ant farm. With a little bit of luck a tunnel might terminate with a nesting cave right against the glass, and if so, an opportunity will be afforded for the gerbil keeper to intimately observe even the nesting and brooding behavior. Tunneling against the glass can be encouraged if black paper is taped onto the outside of the glass for a while. Once the tunnels are dug, the paper can be removed, and then most of the gerbils' underground activities can be observed. After a few minutes the paper should be replaced on the glass, or else the gerbils, who seemingly enjoy a modest amount of privacy, will begin to dig new tunnels and probably dig them out toward the center of the tank, away from the prying eyes of their keeper!

An interesting observation we have made is that even though the gerbils create an intricate network of tunnels under the soil surface, they very often prefer to build the nest and brood the young in a corner of the tank up on the soil surface. This seems especially true if they are given plenty of nesting material such as straw, twigs, torn rags, wood chips, etc. We have also observed that tunneling activities never seem to stop. The gerbils almost constantly rearrange the underground terrain, digging new

Opposite: *Although gerbils are inquisitive and friendly animals, they do require some privacy.*

tunnels and filling in old ones. The network of tunnels never appears to be the same on any two consecutive days, although the entrances and exits to and from the surface don't seem to be changed as often as the tunnels themselves are.

The soil-filled aquarium setup has one big disadvantage to the gerbil owner, but that disadvantage is probably a great advantage to the gerbils themselves. Gerbils cannot be handled very often in this setup, for it is not as easy to catch them as it is when they are housed in a metal cage. This is probably so because here they just aren't handled as often—there is no need, since the litter doesn't have to be changed—and so they don't become as tame. In the soil-filled aquarium gerbils definitely can be trained to come to your hand, but in the process they can escape into their burrows if they are inadvertently frightened, and this they cannot do in a metal cage. Of course, you can always collapse the tunnels, but that's not being very kind to the gerbils, and it could injure or kill them. Furthermore, this will teach them to fear a human hand—this they will remember!

TEMPERATURE AND HUMIDITY

There is no difficulty in maintaining the correct temperature in a gerbil cage.

Whatever temperature suits the gerbil keeper suits the gerbils as well. Even wide variations in temperature will not cause gerbils to hibernate. They can tolerate temperatures of over 100°F. and temperatures below freezing (32°F.). In their natural environment they experience this kind of temperature variation every year. However, even though they are tolerant of a wide range of temperature fluctuations, this does not mean that they should be deliberately subjected to them. They can comfortably tolerate a range variance from 60 to 85°F. every day as long as the change is gradual. Greater daily temperature variations could cause gerbils to become quite ill. A normal room temperature of 65 to 72°F. seems to suit gerbils just fine. Because of the gerbils' normal body heat, the internal cage temperature may remain a degree or two higher than the room temperature. This depends upon the type of cage, its location in the room and the relative humidity. But whether the cage temperature is a few degrees higher or lower than the room temperature does not matter. What does matter is that the gerbils should not be subjected to sudden temperature changes of any great difference such as 20 or 25 degrees. In other words, keep the cage away from drafty windows and doors. During the

Variety is important in the gerbil diet. Different foods provide different necessary nutrients, and they help keep the gerbil interested in life.

winter, if the gerbils are going to be taken outdoors, as they would be to transport them somewhere, be sure to wrap the cage either with newspapers or with an old blanket to avoid exposing the gerbils to chilling drafts. Gerbils are definitely exposed to freezing temperatures in the wild, but down in their burrows they are at least protected from cold drafts. It is the drafts and sudden temperature drops, not the cool temperatures themselves, that cause gerbils to become ill.

Humidity control is not at all necessary for keeping gerbils successfully. Even though in nature they live in arid, sandy regions, a relative humidity of 85%

or more will not harm them at all. The only problem caused by a relative humidity higher than about 50% is that the gerbils' fur, instead of lying smoothly against the body, tends to stand out and become matted. Gerbils seem to compensate for this somewhat by grooming themselves more often in a moister atmosphere then they do in a drier atmosphere.

LIGHT

Because gerbils have relatively large eyes compared to those of most other kinds of common pet rodents, and because they come from desert habitats and live in burrows, many people just assume that they are nocturnal creatures. It is true that most desert mammals rest and hide during the day and prowl and hunt for food at dusk or during the night. While it is probably true that gerbils follow that schedule to some degree in the wild, and while it is also true that many strictly nocturnal creatures remain nocturnal in captivity, it is not true that gerbils are nocturnal in captivity. The activity of gerbils is cyclic, peaking at about midnight, but they take frequent rest periods during the day and during the night. Therefore a normal light cycle of twelve to eighteen hours, the same light cycle that is comfortable for the gerbil keeper, is fine for the gerbils. Changing their light cycle will not affect their

behavior very much. If, for instance, their light cycle is reversed, they quickly adjust and reverse the timing of their activity peaks.

It is not necessary and probably not even desirable to have artificial illumination directly over and close to the gerbil cage. Normal room light from overhead lights, table lamps and windows is more than sufficient.

FOODS, FEEDING AND WATER

Very little information is available on the specific nutrient requirements of gerbils, but for the purpose of keeping them as pets, very little specific information is needed.

Nutritional deficiencies in gerbils can be avoided the same way they are avoided in fishes, other pets and even in humans—make sure they get a well-varied diet. This is known as the shotgun approach—with so many items in the diet, most of the nutritional needs are bound to be covered. As unprofessional as it sounds, it does work. In fact, it works so well that many laboratories using gerbils in research take the same approach. Getting gerbils to eat a variety of foods i s no problem. In

Opposite: *A cinnamon white spot and an agouti. Gerbils enjoy "natural" settings; placing plants in the gerbil captive environment, however, is useless and may be dangerous.*

fact, they'll eat almost anything you offer them.

Commercial diets do have research behind them, and they contain a balance of minerals, vitamins and other substances needed by gerbils and other small research animals. Commercially available are rat, mouse, hamster and rabbit pelleted foods in addition to gerbil foods. Because gerbils have been kept as pets for a shorter period than hamsters and rabbits there are fewer pelleted foods specifically manufactured for gerbil consumption. However, gerbils seem to thrive quite well on pelleted foods designed for feeding to rats, mice, hamsters and rabbits. These food pellets are rather hard, so in addition to fulfilling the gerbil's nutritional needs they also fulfill their need for material to gnaw upon, for that is exactly how gerbils eat these pellets; they gnaw on them. They pick them up with the forefeet, or hands if you prefer, and more or less turn them against the incisor teeth as they gnaw away. In addition to providing gerbils with a balanced diet, these foods apparently aid gerbils in keeping their incisor teeth short and sharpened.

As dry as these foods may seem, apparently they do contain some moisture, for even on a steady diet of these hard pellets gerbils still require very little water.

On the contrary, commercial monkey pellets do not meet gerbils' needs, for they are much softer than rat or hamster pellets and contain more water than gerbils should have if the food is used on a daily basis. Furthermore, monkey pellets don't provide for the gerbils' gnawing needs. We have observed gerbils on a steady diet of monkey pellets and noted that their feces were not of the usual hard, dry consistency, and the bedding in their cages needed to be changed more often, so presumably they urinated more often than they normally do. These differences in their waste products were probably related to the moisture content of their diet, for when the same gerbils were put on a diet of rat pellets their waste products returned to normal. In addition, they perked up in their behavior and the appearance of their fur improved. These changes may also have been possibly related to the specific ingredients of the two types of foods as well as their moisture content.

While adolescent and adult gerbils seem to do quite well on a steady diet of the hard pellets, weanlings and young juveniles don't do quite as well with them. The food seems to be just a bit too hard for these youngsters. These young gerbils look quite funny gnawing away on food pellets that are almost as big as the animals

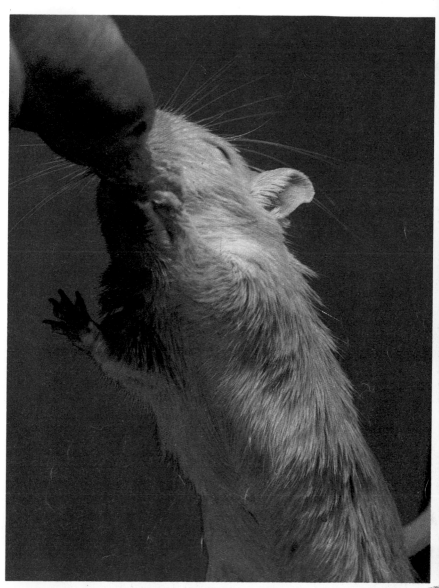

A tame pet gerbil will eagerly accept food from its master's hand. One must be careful, however, not to overfeed nor spoil the animal.

themselves. They soon learn to look for smaller pieces that have been broken off and dropped by feeding adults. It helps if the gerbil keeper takes some time to break some of the pellets into smaller pieces. To help these young gerbils get enough nutrition while their teeth and jaw muscles are growing larger and stronger, their diet can be supplemented with mixed grains, seeds and rolled oats.

To eliminate dietary monotony and ensure a better dietary balance, there are other suitable foods that can be used to supplement the gerbil's diet. They do have a need for vegetable matter and moisture. To fulfill this

A pair of three-week-old babies at play. Note the intent expression of the gerbil facing the sunflower seeds.

A cinnamon female gerbil keeping an eye on her six-week-old daughter.

need they can be given medium-size lettuce leaves a few times a week. Although lettuce is expensive, feeding it to gerbils is not; for gerbils eagerly eat the wilted outer leaves of the lettuce head as readily as they eat the prime inner leaves, and most people usually throw out the wilted outer leaves. They also eat the core of the lettuce head, and that too is usually scrap as far as humans are concerned. Gerbils can also occasionally be given pieces of carrot, celery, cabbage, broccoli, turnip or almost any other item of produce. It is possible to acquire these vegetables free by making a deal with your local produce salesman.

Gerbils relish most of the scrap that fruit and vegetable stores throw away. Another vegetable item that is a favorite of many gerbils and is also free for the taking for at least part of the year is dandelion greens, and anybody who owns a home and cares for a lawn knows how readily available dandelions are. There is only one possible problem in using dandelion greens as a food supplement for gerbil—they store toxins from pesticides and herbicides, and these could poison the gerbils. Don't use dandelions if they have been sprayed with weed-killers or if the ground they are growing in has been fertilized with fertilizers containing herbicides. It is safest to get dandelion greens from an unused field or a pasture where there has been no spraying.

All of these fresh vegetables contain a lot of moisture, so they should be given to the gerbils quite sparingly; otherwise they

These two animals represent both ends of the gerbil genetic spectrum. **Below:** *A lovely albino gerbil.* **Opposite:** *A striking black gerbil.*

Above: *A wide variety of gerbil houses are available at your local pet shop.* **Opposite:** *A gerbil might make a nice gift for an animal lover, but one should always keep in mind that a responsible pet owner plans carefully for the arrival of any new animal.*

could cause digestive and elimination problems including soft feces and excessive urination.

Another excellent dietary supplement for gerbils is sunflower seeds. They are quite inexpensive to purchase, but if you have an inclination toward gardening, it can be fun to grow your own. Sunflower seeds are not only a good dietary supplement, but they also make excellent occasional treats, for gerbils seem to love them and will even overeat if given too many of them—they don't usually overeat most foods. In addition to making your gerbils ecstatically happy,

Below: *A healthy diet will keep a gerbil's coat healthy and its eyes bright. It will also create a longer, happier life.* **Opposite:** *Sunflower seeds are probably the favorite food of most gerbils. They are, however, fattening; therefore, they should be given in moderation.*

sunflower seeds serve several other purposes. For one, their husks are removed by the gerbils in such a way that they can be used as nesting material. Secondly, sunflower seeds are a useful treat in taming and training gerbils. Gerbil keepers frequently use them as a reward for good or correct behaviors.

If gerbils are being kept in a soil environment, sunflower seeds often escape their scrutiny. These seeds will eventually germinate, and when they do gerbils waste no time mowing them down and eating them. In one of our large gerbil colonies we once named the dominant male our Gentleman Farmer, for at times it almost seemed as though he intentionally planted the sunflower seeds and then harvested the crop!

Like fresh vegetables, sunflower seeds must be given to gerbils only on a limited basis, not

Gerbil treats, such as nut sticks, are available in pet shops. They make wonderful rewards for gerbils that are being tamed.

Gerbils provide their owners with much amusement when they eat sunflower seeds.

because of their high water content as in the vegetables, but because of their high fat content. Gerbils are possibly even more prone than humans to developing high blood serum cholesterol levels and may do so even on a diet containing a normal amount of fat. Gerbils readily store fat, and on a diet consisting of a lot of sunflower seeds they will become quite obese. This may interfere with reproduction, since one of the places that fat tends to accumulate in gerbils is around the ovaries. There is also no reason to believe that obesity in gerbils does not cause for them the same kinds of problems it causes in humans—circulatory and respiratory ailments. Because of the apparent health hazards

involved, it behooves the gerbil keeper to use sunflower seeds only as an occasional treat for the gerbils and not as a regular part of the diet.

How much food to give gerbils is always a question posed by new gerbil owners. With the occasional exception of sunflower seeds, gerbils do not often overeat, so there is usually no need to worry about overfeeding them. Gerbils do not store food in cheek pouches like hamsters do, but they are, nonetheless, food hoarders. Very often gerbils take their food back to their nest or into a tunnel to eat it. They also store extra food there. If you can give your gerbils some attention every day, it is a good idea not to give them more food than they can consume in one day, for stored foods can spoil and sicken gerbils in addition to spoiling the substrate in the cage a lot sooner. This is especially true in a soil environment where rainwater may drain into the gerbils' food cache and soak into the food, making it more susceptible to spoilage. One laboratory claims that the average gerbil living in a colony consisting of gerbils of all ages consumes about one-fourth to one-fifth of an ounce of food per day. If you have only adult gerbils, give them a little more per gerbil. However, if the colony consists of only two adults and seven one- or two-month-old pups, give them less than one-fifth of an ounce of food per day per gerbil. With a little bit of experience, you'll learn how much food to give them.

As far as presenting food to gerbils is concerned, the construction of some cages makes feeding easy, for the covers contain a built-in food hopper. You can put a one-day supply of food in the hopper or you can fill it with up to a two-week supply, depending upon how many gerbils are in the cage. There is an opening at the bottom of the hopper that allows a gerbil sitting upright to remove one piece of food at a time. Gerbils don't fight over food very often, but once in a while an overzealous eater must be pushed away from the hopper opening by another

gerbil. If your gerbils are being kept in a soil-filled aquarium, the food may simply be placed on a flat spot on the soil surface or in a shallow dish placed on top of the soil. The food is not likely to remain in the dish very long, but if the gerbils have constructed a hilly terrain, as they often do, at least the food won't roll into the tunnels before the gerbils have had a chance to find it. If they roll it in later, at least they will know where it is.

Gerbils have an unusual system of water metabolism. They have a tremendous tolerance to dehydration and rehydration. It has been observed in the wild that gerbils have absolutely no need for water other then that which they extract from their food. On a steady diet of rat pellets gerbils will get some water, but not enough. On such a diet they must be given some supplemental water. However, if they are given a few small- to medium-size lettuce leaves and perhaps a small piece of carrot or turnip every week, they do not need to be given any water at all. They will extract all they need from the vegetables.

Opposite: *A father gerbil with his babies. A male gerbil seldom hinders the female in childrearing. Some males may even help with caring for the pups.*

It is often quite difficult for us humans to accept the gerbil's lack of need for much water, for we ourselves need a lot of water, as do most of the animals we see around us, including many gerbil-like creatures. Therefore, in order to accommodate our own desire for our pets not to be thirsty, there is no harm in providing your gerbils with a watering bottle, even if they are getting fresh vegetables, for they will not drink more than they need anyhow.

The water is usually kept in a small bottle that is fitted with a cork or rubber stopper that has a glass or stainless steel sipping tube protruding from it. If you have a standard metal cage, the watering bottle anchors to the outside of it and the sipping tube, which is usually bent at a slight angle, protrudes into the cage

Dove and cinnamon gerbils. Gerbils spend part of their day at play, with the younger animals doing so more often.

Although gerbils do not require much water in their diet, it is a good idea to provide each cage with a water bottle. Different types are available at pet shops.

between the bars. If an aquarium is used to house the gerbils, the watering bottle can be placed on top of the cover so that the drinking tube protrudes into the tank. The bottle should be located so that the gerbils can drink from an upright position. This means that the tip of the tube must be no closer than four inches from the bottom or the soil surface. If there are young gerbils present, the tube should be hung a little bit lower or a second bottle mounted in a lower position should be used.

Above: *Since the gerbil is an alert animal with good eyesight, sense of hearing, and sense of smell, it is usually aware of its owner's presence.* **Opposite:** *Holding a gerbil by its tail is not harmful, as long as care is taken not to hold the animal this way for too long a time.*

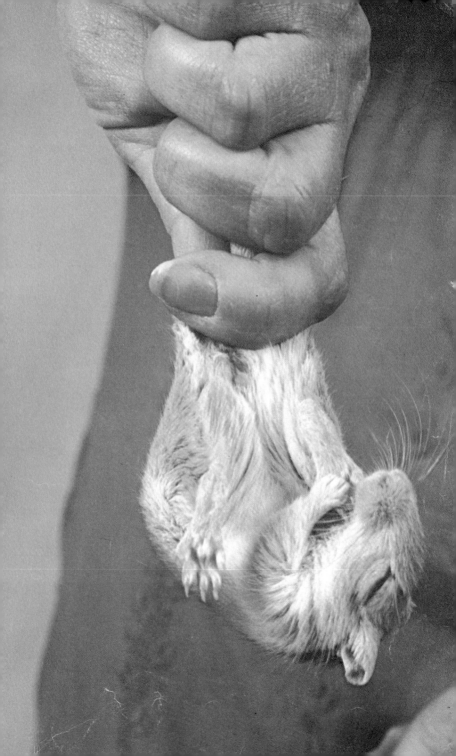

Handling Gerbils

The gerbil's docile nature has been discussed, and hopefully you were not led into believing that gerbils do not bite, for under some circumstances they do. However, it takes a lot more punishment or abuse to get a gerbil to bite than it does any other type of pet rodent. About the only thing that causes gerbils to bite, short of intentional abuse, is careless handling, and most careless handling arises out of fear by the handler. Knowing how to properly pick up a gerbil and how to hold it carefully will help most handlers overcome their fear of being bitten or of hurting the animal and will thus reduce the chances of being bitten to almost none.

Your first encounter with your new gerbils is probably the most important, for if you hurt or frighten them they are not likely to forget the shape and smell of your hand for some time to come. The first thing to do is merely present your hand to the gerbils when they are in their cage. This gives them a chance to explore your hand in their territory and on their terms. The hand should not be presented open, for fingertips and the skin between the fingers are the easiest places for gerbils to chomp! Always, even after the gerbils are tamed and accustomed to you, present your hand with the fist closed and the palm down. This gives the gerbils no easy place to bite into if they become frightened. Allow them to sniff and explore your hand for a few minutes so that they can become familiar with its smell, texture, shape and feel. At first they will sniff your hand, and then they may accidentally or intentionally bump or touch it. For the first few minutes your hand should not be moved, and then it should be very slowly moved about for a few seconds and perhaps even rotated. With the palm still down and the fist still clenched, allow the gerbils to continue exploring and even climb up on your hand if they can, although they probably will not climb up until the hand is opened. They may even lick your hand. Don't let this bother you, for their saliva may be more germ-free than yours!

Once this first introduction is successful, you may slowly, with your palm up, begin to unfold your fingers. More exploration will occur. The open palm is more conducive to stimulating the gerbil into climbing up on your hand than is a closed fist. You will sense when the gerbils are comfortable with the presence of your hand.

Now, once again, begin to move your hand around slowly. If a gerbil happens to be sitting on your palm, don't let that stop you.

Opposite: *A young black gerbil. Gerbils do not bite very often, but they may do so if they are provoked.*

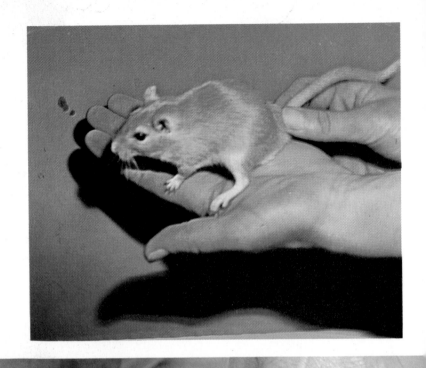

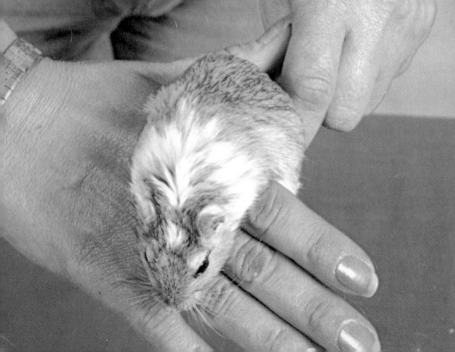

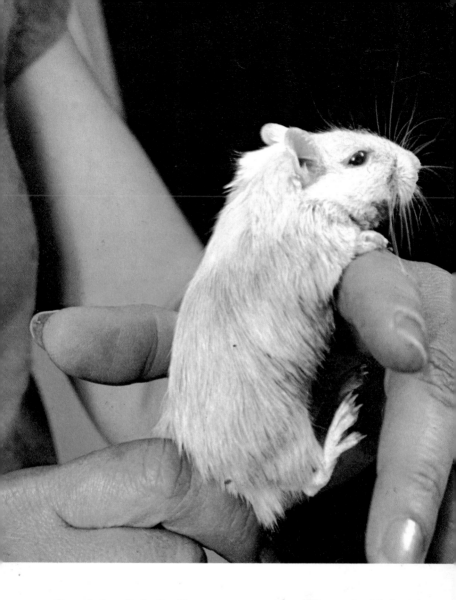

Opposite top: *During handling, one can support a gerbil by cupping it in the palm of one's hand.* **Opposite bottom and above:** *One can also nestle the animal on the back of one hand and shield it with the other. With experience, you will find that it is not necessary to grip the animal too tightly.*

Handling Gerbils

Lift the gerbil up in the air. If it hasn't yet climbed onto your hand, you can encourage this by slowly and gently forcing your fingers under them.

Now let the gerbil hop off your hand and slowly withdraw your hand from the cage. Remember— *no sudden movements!* Move around the cage to let the gerbils know you are still there. After a few minutes, put your hand back into the cage and start the introduction all over again. By the time the second introduction is over the gerbil is usually ready for a more intimate encounter. However, if you are not yet comfortable with the thought of having more intimate contact with your gerbil, then continue to repeat the hand introduction until you are completely relaxed about it.

You should now be ready to pick your gerbil up, and there are two ways to do this. The first way has already begun. Encourage whichever gerbil seems to be most interested to climb onto your hand and gently lift it out of the cage. All of this should be done as close to the floor as possible to minimize injuries should the animal fall from your hand. Once you've come this far with no mishaps, you'll be pretty much free to handle the gerbil as often and however you wish (within reason, of course).

The other way to lift a gerbil is to slowly and gently but firmly grab the base of the gerbil's tail between your thumb and forefinger and slowly lift the gerbil up in a head-down position. Gerbils usually don't mind this kind of handling as long as you are gentle with them. Once the gerbil is lifted out of the cage, place the palm of your other hand under the animal and gently lower it onto your hand. The only way that this will become a traumatic experience for the gerbil is if you grab the tail anywhere along its rear half. If this is how the animal is being held, a slight twisting motion by the gerbil will greatly increase the torque on its spine and probably cause it some pain. This can lead to panic and more twisting until the skin virtually rips off the gerbil's tail and the animal falls to the floor. It is entirely possible that, like the lizards that give up their tail, this is an escape mechanism for gerbils living in the wild. However, it should not be allowed to happen to gerbils living in captivity. The gerbil may grow some new covering on the tail, but it will remember this negative incident for a long time. When grabbing a gerbil by the tail, your fingers should be as close to its rump as possible. This will almost always prevent any discomfort to the gerbil and will effectively eliminate most panic reactions.

A one-handed restraint can be used on the gerbil by grasping it

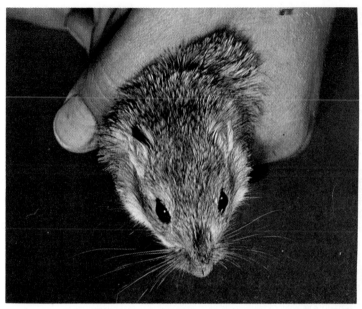

This is one of the proper ways to hold a gerbil. Always be sure to support the animal's body and to make it as comfortable as possible.

around the shoulder area with your whole hand and allowing its head to protrude from the circle formed by your thumb and forefinger. However, in such a restraint the gerbil may attempt to wiggle free. If, in this or any other grasp, the gerbil is turned belly up, it will inevitably struggle to get free of the grasp. This grasp should only be used when complete restraint is needed, such as during examination of a wound or during treatment for an ailment.

Because gerbils love to explore new things and places, they may crawl up your sleeve or down your collar. If the thought of this happening bothers you, then before picking the gerbils up make sure your collar is tightly buttoned and your sleeves rolled up tightly.

Both you and the gerbil can have a lot of fun if the gerbil is allowed to climb into your shirt pocket or perhaps into a cup. There are few small pet animals that are more endearing than a gerbil with its head sticking out of a shirt pocket.

If your gerbils escape, there is really no reason or need to panic, for they are easier to recapture than any other small rodent. The

Above: *Holding a gerbil loosely in one hand is not safe. It can easily escape.* **Opposite:** *In this manner of holding a gerbil, internal injuries are possible; one may tend to squeeze harder as the animal struggles to escape.*

first thing to do is immediately close the doors of the room the gerbils are in. Actually, it is a good idea to close the doors before you take the gerbils out of their cage in the first place. That way if they escape, one step in their recapture is already accomplished, and you won't have to chase them from room to room.

What makes gerbils so easy to recapture is their docile nature and innate curiosity, and if you don't panic, you can capitalize on that curiosity. Don't make any sudden movements or loud noises. Slowly, on your hands and knees, look under every piece of furniture until you locate the escapees. Then, with a closed hand, slowly go through all the motions of an introduction until you can either grab the gerbils by the tail base or lift them onto your

If you are going to hold a gerbil by the tail, be sure to hold the very base of the tail.

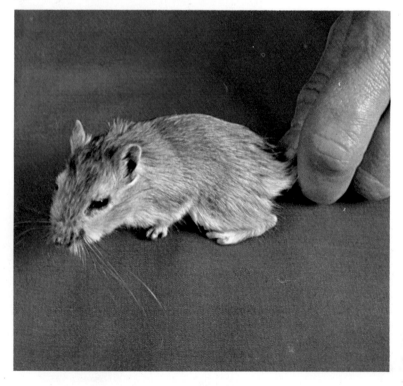

It may be a good idea to reward your pet gerbil after a successful handling session. Treats such as these are available at your local pet shop.

open palm. Sounds easy, doesn't it? It is if you don't panic. If, in the process of escaping, the gerbils have been frightened, it is best to just sit very still in the middle of the floor until the gerbils come out of hiding on their own accord. By then their fright is gone, and the old extended hand trick will work easily.

Sometimes a familiar sight or odor will draw the escaped gerbils out of hiding, so if nothing else

works try placing their cage, with the door open, on the floor and then leaving the room and closing the door behind you. The chances are pretty good that when you return an hour or two later the gerbils will be in their cage, especially if you've already had them for a few months.

Above all, remember that panic accomplishes nothing other than making the job of recapture exceedingly difficult!

Opposite top: *This gerbil is in the process of marking a spot with its scent gland.*
Opposite bottom: *Disposal of soiled litter and used nesting material is easily accomplished in a cage that is equipped with a removable bottom tray.* **Above:** *A white or albino gerbil alongside a normal gerbil. Note the lack of pigmentation in different parts of the body, including the eyes.*

Gerbil Health

Of all the rodents or other small animals commonly kept as pets, gerbils seem to be the hardiest and most disease-free. While rats, mice and most other small mammals kept in captivity have diseases that are peculiar to each alone, no diseases peculiar to gerbils alone have so far been discovered. Gerbils also seem to be immune to some of the diseases that are prevalent in other rodents.

Colds, pneumonia and diarrhea are ailments that gerbils occasionally suffer from. Weanling pups more than adolescent or adult gerbils are susceptible to the bacterial infections that cause diarrhea. These infections do not seem to be highly contagious and can be treated by adding 0.3 grams of tetracycline hydrochloride (a wide-spectrum antibiotic) to each 100 ml. of drinking water.

Gerbils are susceptible to Tyzzer's disease, although the disease is far less prevalent in gerbils than it is in other rodents. Gerbils having the disease are lethargic, they don't eat much, they have rough fur and they lose weight rather rapidly. This disease is contagious to other gerbils, but it does not cause many deaths among them. Wide-spectrum antibiotics often cure this disease too.

The symptoms of a cold are quite similar to those described for Tyzzer's disease. However, like most diseases in gerbils, the cold will run its course, with fatalities being very rare.

Bacterial skin infections have been reported in gerbils. Lesions or sores first show up around the nose, and for this reason the disease has become known as red-nose. Red-nose disease eventually spreads to the legs and the belly region. Young gerbils are more susceptible to red-nose than adults are. Tetracycline in the drinking water and dips in disinfectants such as nitrofurazone have produced some positive results in curing this disease.

Gerbils, like almost any mammal, can be attacked by tapeworms, mites, fleas and many other external and internal parasites. Getting rid of these various parasites is not easy, but preventing them from attacking the gerbils in the first place is quite easy. Simply keep the gerbils' cages very clean and make sure they get a variety of good quality foods. This helps keep their resistance to external and internal parasites and diseases quite high. There are other diseases, some curable and some uncurable, that occasionally show up in gerbils,

Opposite: *A healthy gerbil is one that is aware of and interested in its surroundings.*

Opposite top: *Physical features, such as large size and good health, are always considered in a potential breeder along with a desired genetic quality, such as albinism in this gerbil.* **Opposite bottom:** *Pied or broken color pattern may be common in other small mammals, but it is not often encountered in gerbils.* **Above:** *A large litter of gerbils is preferred by breeders; those pups that fail to satisfy the show standard are culled.*

but they are so rare that there is little value in describing them. By and large, though, gerbils are the most disease-free pet rodents. Abnormalities such as kinked tails, hairless tails and hairless feet and legs sometimes manifest themselves in gerbils that have been inbred for a number of generations. Gerbils so affected are usually smaller than normal, don't reproduce as well and generally don't live nearly as long as normal gerbils, although they do very often live to adulthood. Apparently the visible external abnormalities in these gerbils are only the tip of the iceberg, so to speak. They probably have many internal systemic abnormalities also; otherwise they would grow and reproduce normally and would

live out a normal life span. Although some of these abnormalities could be the result of a poor diet, that is certainly not the case when gerbils on a normal nutritious diet show these defects.

Inbreeding, the apparent cause of these abnormalities, is the breeding of animals that are closely related, for example father to daughter, mother to son or, more commonly, sister to brother. If you wish to keep your strain of gerbils healthy and flourishing, such closely related matings should not be allowed to occur, or at least should not occur very often. They can be eliminated right from the beginning by initially selecting your males and females from different sources. This will usually ensure that the gerbils are

Do not hesitate to call your veterinarian if you feel there is something wrong with your gerbil. A few hours may make a difference between life and death.

Note the lovely long tail of the gerbil. It is believed that the tail detaches from the body when the gerbil is attacked by a predator; this allows the gerbil to escape. Do not forget, however, that tail injuries are quite painful.

not brothers and sisters. You can continue to eliminate inbreeding by not allowing the members of subsequent litters to breed with one another. One generation of inbreeding will not usually cause problems, but the problems will start to crop up by the second or third generation of brother to sister matings. To keep your gerbil colony thriving without these problems, simply introduce some stock from a different source at each generation or at least at every other generation.

All in all, gerbils are about the easiest small mammals to care for. In fact, they require so little care to remain healthy and flourishing that normal care for gerbils might be considered neglect for most other small animals.

Left: *Gerbils are very vulnerable immediately after birth and can be expected to die if they are abandoned by their mother.* **Opposite:** *A pregnant female will require a richer diet than the usual for the development of the young and for lactation later.*

Breeding Your Gerbils

Before breeding a pair of gerbils, be sure that both the male and the female are in excellent health.

Breeding gerbils is not very difficult, although they don't always breed as readily as pet rats, mice, hamsters or rabbits. More often than not, however, it is almost impossible to prevent them from breeding.

The first step, of course, is to make sure that you have a male and a female. Once gerbils have reached puberty they are quite easy to sex. Hold them up by the base of the tail and examine the genital region. The scrotum of the male appears as a black area under the base of the tail. The female, of course, lacks a scrotum and hence lacks the darkened area in the genital region. While mature males are usually a bit

larger than mature females, making this observation is not a very reliable way to determine their sex, for you could have an exceptionally large or small male or female or there could be an age difference between them which would account for their difference in size.

Some observers of captive gerbils claim them to be monogamous. This observation is no doubt based on the fact that when several pairs are kept together there seems to be no exchanging of mates. The facts are, however, that gerbils are not truly monogamous creatures, even though they apparently tend toward monogamy in captivity. In fact, it is possible to establish breeding lines in gerbils by mating offspring to their parents.

Although not truly monogamous, gerbils tend to be selective. Any randomly selected male and female cannot always be paired, especially if they are fully matured adults when they are first put together by themselves, even if they were both selected from the same colony. With young specimens the chances of randomly selecting a compatible pair are much better. Young specimens are also always easier to tame and train than mature adults.

In the beginning, pair formation can almost be assured if at least two females and one male are purchased and placed together in the same cage, providing the gerbils are only about eight weeks old at the time of the purchase. If the gerbils are allowed to reach sexual maturity together, they will usually form a pair bond. After the pair is formed, the extra female can usually be left in the cage with no harm coming to her, but once in a rare while the extra female may be harassed and possibly killed, usually by the other female.

Gerbils are polyestrus animals; that is, they do not necessarily breed only during one particular part of the year. In other words, they are not seasonal breeders in captivity, as so many other animals coming from temperate or arctic climates are. Rather, once gerbils reach breeding age, which occurs at about twelve weeks after birth, they breed throughout the year. However, they do seem to reach a reproductive peak around mid-summer and their reproductivity declines to a low point at about mid-winter. During the peak period, litters are usually about 25% larger in number than average and are born at about a 25% greater frequency than average. During the low reproductivity period the birth rate drops to about 25% below average. Very rarely does a litter of gerbils have a skewed sex ratio. Usually they consist of approximately 50% males and 50% females.

The mating of a dove female and a Canadian white spot male.

The female's reproductive life usually lasts for about fifteen months, but toward the end of that period the birth rate declines and the litter size decreases in number. During a female gerbil's reproductive life she bears an average of about seven litters. A male's reproductive life usually outlasts that of a female.

As mentioned earlier, thumping by the male is an intricate part of the mating ritual. If the female is in estrus (physiologically prepared to be fertilized), she responds to the male's thumping by presenting her hindquarters. If she is not in estrus, mating will usually not occur—the female will not allow it. The male usually mounts the estrus female a number of times in quick succession before fertilization actually occurs. He may repeat his thumping behavior between each mounting.

The gestation period of the gerbil is about 25 days. The female can again become

Opposite top: *At the age of two weeks gerbils are fully furred and sighted, but they are still too immature for weaning.* **Opposite bottom:** *Young gerbils can withstand normal handling similar to the methods recommended for adults. Extra caution, however, is recommended.* **Above:** *With growth, the body proportions of this immature white gerbil will change to those of an adult; the tail will be as long or longer than the body and the head proportionally smaller in relation to the body length.*

pregnant during the period in which she is nursing her pups. In fact, some researchers have found that this is when a young fertile female is most likely to become pregnant.

The average litter consists of about five pups. They are born hairless, sightless and almost entirely helpless. At birth the pups usually weigh about three grams and are bright pink in color. After a few days they begin to develop hair, and by the time they are ready to be weaned, which occurs at the age of about twenty days, they have a full coat of fur. Their eyes open at about ten to twelve days of age. At weaning age a gerbil pup's head seems to be disproportionately large for the size of its body. However, as a pup matures the body catches up in its proportional size to the head. Other changes in relative proportions also occur as the gerbil matures. For instance, the tail is quite short at birth, but by the time the gerbil matures the tail is almost as long as the body itself.

For reasons unknown to anyone, small litters consisting of only one or two pups rarely survive. Overall, though, the survival rate of gerbil pups born and cared for in captivity is quite high. Gerbil pups seem to be about as hardy as adults. Once in a great while an entire litter may

die, usually due to maternal neglect or to failure of the female to produce milk, but these occasions are rare. Maternal neglect is more prevalent in females that have just had their first litter and in older females that are past their reproductive prime. Older females sometimes do not lactate very well either.

Among some rodents, cannibalism of the young is quite prevalent. With gerbils, however, even under very crowded conditions cannibalism is very rare. Gerbils generally are excellent parents, and it is not at all uncommon for a male to help herd the pups together and for him to rest with the pups curled up under him. When the pups wander from the nest, which they begin to do at about twelve days of age, the parents, using their teeth, grab them by the loose skin on the back of the neck and transport them back to the nest. Rarely, if ever, does a male interfere with a brooding female. In colonies, females often help one another with their brooding activities, and sometimes they even foster nurse. If pups die before they are weaned, they are usually ignored by the parents rather than eaten, as are dead pups of some rodents. In fact, with captive gerbils it is not uncommon for the parents to bury their deceased pups.

Index

Average litter size, 92
Bacterial skin infections, 80
Cage: height, 36; construction, 36; litter, 36; moisture, 43; soil, 40
Cannibalism, 92
Classification, 12
Dandelion greens, 58
Davidson, Professor, 19
Dexterity, 32
Digging, 28
Egyptian gerbil, 13, 15
Food pellets, 50
Gestation period, 89
Gnawing, 28
Grooming, 32
Housing, 34
Humidity, 47
Inbreeding, 84
Indian gerbil, 16
Jerboa, 11

Jerusalem gerbil, 13
King gerbil, 14
Libyan gerbil, 13
Light, 48
Mating, 89
Namib Paeba gerbil, 16
Pair formation, 88
Parasites, 80
Przewalski's gerbil, 17
Pygmy (dwarf) gerbil, 14
Recapturing, 76
Reproductive life, 89
Schwentker, Dr. Victor, 19
Scratching, 28
Sexing, 87
Sunflower seeds, 60
Temperature, 46
Thumping, 25, 29, 89
Tyzzer's disease, 80
Vegetables, 53
Water metabolism, 62

Gerbils make wonderful pets for the whole family. They appeal to the young and old alike.

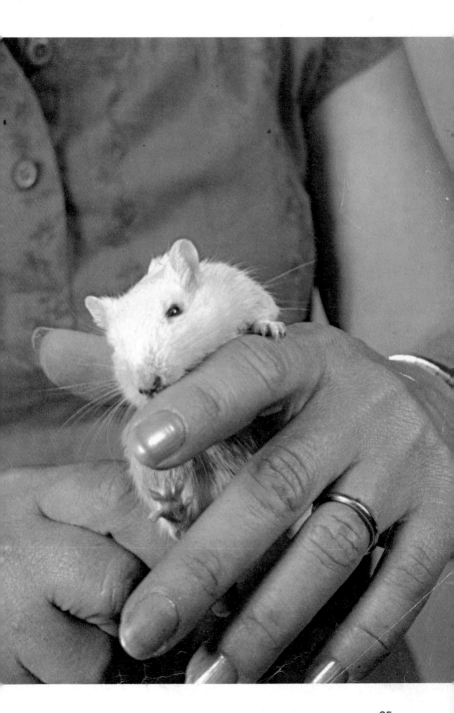

GERBILS
KW-037